THE
NBA
A HISTORY OF HOOPS

Published by Creative Education
P.O. Box 227, Mankato, Minnesota 56002
Creative Education is an imprint of The Creative Company
www.thecreativecompany.us

Design and production by Christine Vanderbeek
Art direction by Rita Marshall

Printed by Corporate Graphics in the United States of America

Photographs by Dreamstime (Munktcu), Getty Images (Brian Bapineau/NBAE,
Bill Baptist/NBAE, Andrew D. Bernstein/NBAE, Darren Carroll/Sports Illustrated,
Chris Covatta/NBAE, Scott Cunningham/NBAE, James Drake/Sports Illustrated,
D. Clarke Evans/NBAE, Andy Hayt/NBAE, Andy Hayt/Sports Illustrated, John
Iacono/Sports Illustrated, Fernando Medina/NBAE, Manny Millan/Sports
Illustrated, Panoramic Images, Christian Petersen, SM/AIUEO, Kent Smith/
NBAE, Rocky Widner/NBAE), iStockphoto (Brandon Laufenberg)

Library of Congress Cataloging-in-Publication Data
Hetrick, Hans.
The story of the San Antonio Spurs / by Hans Hetrick.
p. cm. — (The NBA: a history of hoops)
Includes index.
Summary: The history of the San Antonio Spurs professional
basketball team from its start as the Dallas Chaparrals in 1967
to today, spotlighting the franchise's greatest players and moments.
ISBN 978-1-58341-961-8
1. San Antonio Spurs (Basketball team)—History—Juvenile literature.
2. Basketball—Texas—San Antonio—History—Juvenile literature. I. Title. II. Series.
GV885.52.S26H48 2010   796.323'6409764351—dc22   2009036117

CPSIA: 120109 PO1093

First Edition
2 4 6 8 9 7 5 3 1

Page 3: Guard George Hill
Pages 4–5: Spurs celebrating their 2005 championship

THE STORY OF THE
SAN ANTONIO
SPURS

HANS HETRICK

CREATIVE ● EDUCATION

CONTENTS

CHAPTER ONE

LOVE AT FIRST SPUR

As approximately 5,000 Mexican troops attacked a San Antonio mission called the Alamo in 1836, cavalry officer William B. Travis rushed to his post, shouting to his Texan brothers in arms, "No surrender, boys!" Travis and well-known frontiersmen Jim Bowie and Davy Crockett led a group of 184 Texans in the Battle of the Alamo. Against overwhelming odds, the Texans repulsed 2 attacks and held the fort for 13 days before finally being overwhelmed. The Alamo still stands today, and millions of tourists visit San Antonio each year to discover the "never-say-die" spirit that spurred the state of Texas to independence.

Since 1973, San Antonio sports fans have put their indomitable spirit into cheering on a National Basketball Association (NBA) team called the San Antonio Spurs. The Spurs were named after the metal disks that cowboys attach to their boots to help guide their horses. As the sole major professional sports franchise operating in San Antonio, the team has the

Located today in downtown San Antonio, the Alamo is not only a symbol of Texas pride but a major attraction that draws millions of visitors.

full attention of its home city, and its fans prove their loyalty every home game by packing the AT&T Center and shaking the rafters with cheers. San Antonio, however, was not the club's birthplace.

The story of the Spurs actually begins in Dallas, 275 miles northeast of San Antonio. In 1967, the American Basketball Association (ABA) was launched as a rival to the NBA, and one of the original ABA teams was a squad called the Dallas Chaparrals. The Chaparrals, affectionately known to their fans as the "Chaps," took their name from the thorny bushes so common across much of Texas.

The first Chaps lineup was an eccentric group. The team was led by player/coach Cliff Hagen, a physical swingman known for his deadly hook shot. Most of the Chaps' scoring came from center John Beasley and forward Cincinnatus "Cincy" Powell. In the backcourt, Maurice "Toothpick" McHartley, the club's top shooting guard, was famous for playing entire games with a toothpick in his mouth. Although the Chaps put together three winning seasons in their first five years, they won only a single series in the ABA playoffs.

Despite the efforts of the players, the franchise's owners spent little money trying to improve the Chaparrals. They rarely signed their top draft

picks, and Dallas remained a mediocre ABA team. As a result, attendance was atrocious. In 1973, a group of San Antonio investors led by Angelo Drossos, a stockbroker, and B. J. "Red" McCombs, an automotive dealer, saw in the struggling Dallas franchise a chance to bring a major sports team to San Antonio. They agreed to lease the team for three years with an option to buy at the end of the lease. The owners relocated the team to San Antonio and renamed it the Spurs.

San Antonio fans welcomed the Spurs in grandiose fashion. On October 10, 1973, a loud crowd of about 6,000 San Antonians packed HemisFair Arena for the Spurs' home opener against the San Diego Conquistadors. "It's great to play for these people," said Spurs guard Joe Hamilton. "They're rooting for us all the time." San Antonio's faithful following surprised more than just the team's players. The Spurs consistently drew much larger crowds than their NBA counterparts

THE SPURS NEEDED A RULING FROM A FEDERAL COURT AND A LOT OF PATIENCE TO BRING GEORGE GERVIN, "THE ICEMAN," TO SAN ANTONIO. In the early 1970s, Virginia Squires owner Earl Foreman was deep in debt. To keep his ABA franchise afloat, Foreman began selling off his best players. In late 1973, he sold Gervin to the Spurs for $225,000, but getting the highflying forward to San Antonio wasn't easy. ABA commissioner Mike Storen opposed the deal. Without good players, Storen knew, the Squires were headed for disaster, so he told Foreman to give back the money and keep Gervin. But the Spurs didn't want the money; they wanted the Iceman, and they filed a lawsuit against Foreman and Storen to complete the deal. A federal judge immediately granted the Spurs a 10-day injunction (an order to do, or refrain from doing, a certain act until a final ruling is made). The Iceman finally arrived, and to avoid any tricks from Storen or Foreman, the Spurs hid Gervin in a San Antonio hotel until the courts at last ruled in the Spurs' favor.

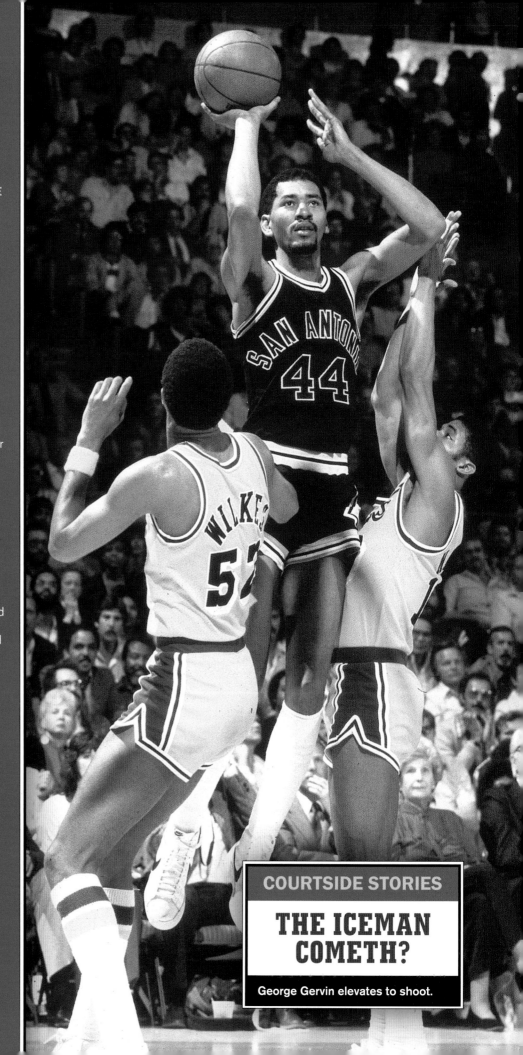

COURTSIDE STORIES

THE ICEMAN COMETH?

George Gervin elevates to shoot.

farther east on Interstate 10, the Houston Rockets. Attendance was so impressive that the San Antonio investors cancelled the lease after the first year and bought the team outright from the stingy owners in Dallas.

During their first year in San Antonio, the Spurs formed a core group of players who would keep them formidable for years to come. The team was built around James Silas, a quick, powerful guard who had earned the nickname "Captain Late" because of his many clutch, late-game performances. "'Si' is a fourth-quarter player," said Spurs coach Bob Bass, who arrived in 1974. "In the final minutes, he gets tougher than the back end of a shooting gallery."

Early in 1973–74, the Spurs picked up center Swen Nater, a reliable rebounder from the Virginia Squires franchise. The Spurs' biggest acquisition that year, however, was "The Iceman," forward George Gervin. Another former Squires star, the unflappable Gervin would lead the Spurs in scoring for 11 of the 12 years he spent with the team.

Silas, Nater, and Gervin thrived in San Antonio's "run-and-gun" offensive scheme. The Spurs' up-tempo style was a hit with fans, too. Attendance continued to rise, and HemisFair Arena became famous

IN THE 1970S AND '80S, THOUSANDS OF KIDS ACROSS AMERICA HAD AN "ICEMAN" POSTER TAPED TO THEIR BEDROOM WALL. On the most famous such poster, George Gervin sat on a throne of ice blocks, a silver basketball in each hand, with "ICEMAN" printed across the bottom. But there was another popular poster, a simple courtside photograph of Gervin's long, skinny body floating toward the rim, the basketball softly rolling off his fingertips. It was the sweetest of shots: the finger roll. Gervin would raise the ball up, the back of his hand facing the rim, and flick the ball in a motion that sent it up in a beautiful arc and then softly down through the net. When asked how he perfected the finger roll, Gervin replied, "I got tired of dunking. I got tired of hitting my wrist. The finger roll was smoother and looked better, and it was easy for me to do with my long arms." Gervin, who earned his nickname because he was so icy cool in clutch moments, was consistently spectacular, averaging at least 21 points per game over almost 12 seasons with the Spurs.

throughout the league for its ear-splitting crowd noise. Although the Spurs posted winning records each of their first three years in San Antonio, they couldn't get past the first round of the ABA playoffs, losing in 1974, 1975, and 1976.

James Silas was drafted—and promptly cut—by the Houston Rockets in 1972; he then joined San Antonio and became a two-time ABA All-Star.

COURTSIDE STORIES

THE BASELINE BUMS

Baseline Bums during a 1975 game.

THE SPURS ARE WELL KNOWN FOR THEIR RABID FAN BASE, AND PERHAPS THE MOST PASSIONATE OF THE BUNCH HAVE BEEN THE BASELINE BUMS, A SMALL GROUP OF SEASON-TICKET HOLDERS WITH SEATS BEHIND THE BASKET. In 1976, the Bums made news during a home game against their ABA Western Division rival, the Denver Nuggets. After a particularly hard-fought loss to San Antonio on March 24, 1976, Nuggets coach Larry Brown told a reporter, "I don't like anything about San Antonio— their coaching staff, their franchise, or their city. The only thing I like about San Antonio is the guacamole salad." When Brown's Nuggets returned to HemisFair Arena later that season, the Baseline Bums were ready. Nuggets forward Gus Gerard remembered that night well. "People were dumping guacamole salad on the players," he said. "When Larry [Brown] went to the locker room, they were pouring beer over his head." Since those rowdy days, the Bums have transformed into a community volunteer organization. Instead of dumping beer on opponents, they help out San Antonio's neediest citizens as representatives of the Spurs.

CHAPTER TWO

HITTING THE NBA RUNNING

I n 1976, the ABA, which was struggling financially, merged with the NBA. Because of their strong team and raucous fan base, the Spurs were one of four teams invited to join the more established league, along with the New York Nets, Denver Nuggets, and Indiana Pacers.

Placed in the Eastern Conference's Central Division, the Spurs hit the court running in their first NBA season. Gervin and multitalented forward Larry Kenon led a high-speed attack that made San Antonio the top-scoring team in the league with an average of 115 points per game. The Spurs finished with a 44–38 record but again failed to advance past the first round of the playoffs, falling to the Boston Celtics.

Before the 1977–78 season, the roof of HemisFair Arena was raised to accommodate an additional 6,000 seats. The team responded to the bigger crowds with its first Central Division title, and Gervin—famed for his elegant finger-roll

A valuable component of San Antonio's highflying offense, Larry Kenon was in his prime in 1978–79, netting 22.1 points per game for the Spurs.

THE QUADRUPLE-DOUBLE (WHEN A PLAYER COMPILES A DOUBLE-DIGIT TOTAL IN FOUR OF FIVE STATISTICAL CATEGORIES INCLUDING POINTS, REBOUNDS, ASSISTS, STEALS, AND BLOCKED SHOTS) IS ONE OF THE RAREST FEATS A BASKETBALL PLAYER CAN ACHIEVE IN THE COURSE OF ONE GAME. In fact, only four quadruple-doubles have been recorded in the history of the NBA. Two of those four are credited to the San Antonio Spurs. The first Spurs player to pull it off was guard Alvin Robertson. On February 18, 1986, Robertson, known for his stifling defense, posted 20 points, 11 rebounds, 10 assists, and 10 steals against the Phoenix Suns—making him the only player ever to achieve a quadruple-double with steals as the fourth category. The second Spurs quadruple-double came from "The Admiral," center David Robinson. On February 17, 1994, he scorched the Detroit Pistons for 34 points, 10 rebounds, 10 assists, and 10 blocked shots. The other two recorded NBA quadruple-doubles belong to two centers, the Chicago Bulls' Nate Thurmond and the Houston Rockets' Hakeem Olajuwon.

COURTSIDE STORIES

DOUBLE QUADRUPLE-DOUBLES

Alvin Robertson heads up the court.

layups—responded by winning the first of his four NBA scoring titles. For most of the season, Gervin and Nuggets swingman David Thompson traded first and second place in the NBA scoring rankings. In an early game on the last day of the season, Thompson jumped ahead of Gervin by netting an amazing 73 points. Later in the day, however, Gervin took the title back for good with a 63-point effort against the New Orleans Jazz, edging Thompson for the title.

After spending two years sidelined by injuries, James Silas entered the 1978–79 season healthy. With Captain Late back in the lineup, Kenon and center Billy "The Whopper" Paultz shone in the frontcourt, but the Iceman still played the starring role. "I consider the game won

Although center Billy Paultz (left) was never a true superstar, he put together a solid 15-year pro career, thanks largely to his tough defense.

when Ice has his hands on the ball," said Paultz. The Spurs claimed another division title and then won their first NBA playoff series, advancing to the 1979 Eastern Conference finals to face the Washington Bullets. San Antonio jumped out to a three-games-to-one series lead, but the Bullets stormed back and won the final three games, including a 107–105 thriller in Game 7.

In 1980, the Spurs moved to the Midwest Division of the Western Conference and continued their winning ways, capturing the division title three years in a row. In 1981–82, Spurs players brought home a slew of individual statistical honors. Gervin claimed his last scoring title with 32.3 points per game, guard Johnny Moore won the NBA assists title with 9.6 per game, and center George Johnson won the blocked shots title by rejecting 3.1 shots a night. Their efforts propelled the Spurs to the Western Conference finals, where they were swept by star center Kareem Abdul-Jabbar and the Los Angeles Lakers.

The Spurs were primed for a championship run in 1982–83. Before the season, San Antonio beefed up its roster by trading with the Bulls for 7-foot-2 center Artis Gilmore, one of the NBA's most physically imposing players. With Gilmore providing muscle and Gervin and fellow forward Mike Mitchell spearheading the offense, the Spurs won a team-record

53 games in 1982–83. They advanced to the conference finals again, but their championship hopes were dashed by the Lakers for a second straight year.

The Spurs then went into a tailspin. In 1984, they missed the playoffs for the first time in their NBA history. A year later, they returned to the postseason but lost in the first round to the Nuggets. Age, it seemed, had caught up with the Spurs. Deciding to rebuild, San Antonio traded Gervin to the Bulls, ending an exciting chapter in Spurs history.

Young guard Alvin Robertson was called upon to fill the void in San Antonio. "The Spurs were always known as a high-scoring offensive team led by Ice," said the team's new coach, Cotton Fitzsimmons. "But we needed toughness and quickness. Alvin gave us that look." Robertson met the challenge, earning both All-Star status and the NBA's Defensive Player of the Year award in 1985–86. Still, San Antonio struggled, posting the first of four straight losing seasons.

CHAPTER THREE

THE ADMIRAL COMES ABOARD

San Antonio's 28–54 record in 1986–87 gave the team the top overall pick in the 1987 NBA Draft. With it, the Spurs selected David Robinson, a 7-foot-1 center from the United States Naval Academy. Even though Robinson would be obligated to serve in the navy for two years after graduation, the Spurs knew he was worth the wait. In the meantime, San Antonio continued to struggle, posting losing records in both 1987–88 and 1988–89.

When Robinson was released from his naval duties in 1989, the Spurs were prepared to win. Having already brought in Larry Brown as the new head coach in 1988, San Antonio now overhauled its roster. Robertson was shipped to the Milwaukee Bucks for All-Star forward Terry Cummings. The Spurs also sent guard Johnny Dawkins and forward Jay Vincent to the

Terry Cummings (top) gave the Spurs six seasons' worth of dogged low-post effort, even as knee problems began to hamper him.

Philadelphia 76ers for speedy guard Maurice Cheeks and forward David

Wingate, and with the third pick of the 1989 NBA Draft, they landed

versatile forward Sean Elliott. All told, there were 9 new faces on the

1989–90 Spurs' 12-man roster. The new-look Spurs jelled more quickly

than anyone could have expected, increasing their win total by 35 over

the previous year to set a record for the biggest one-season improvement

in NBA history.

Although San Antonio ended that season with a heartbreaking, three-
point overtime loss to the Portland Trail Blazers in round two of the
playoffs, hope had been restored. Robinson, nicknamed "The Admiral"
because of his naval background, used his remarkable agility to become
an instant star, scoring 24.3 points a game his rookie season. "He has the
talent all us big guys only hope and dream for," said Spurs backup center
Caldwell Jones. "No other big guy I've ever seen is anywhere near as
quick and fast as he is."

Flanked by Cummings and Elliott, Robinson grew more dominant in
the seasons that followed, becoming a perennial All-Star by averaging
more than 20 points and 10 rebounds a game. The Spurs continued to

rack up wins in the early '90s and make the playoffs, but they consistently fell short of a championship. Critics began to accuse the team's leaders—particularly the easygoing Robinson—of lacking the "killer instinct" needed to win tough playoff games.

n 1993, San Antonio made a move to bring some fire to the lineup, trading Elliott to the Pistons for intense forward Dennis Rodman. Robinson and Rodman could not have been more different in both personality and playing style. Robinson was one of the league's most strait-laced players; Rodman was covered with tattoos and dyed his hair wild colors. Robinson was known for his graceful style and offensive skills; Rodman was known for his scrappy style and defensive tenacity. The only thing the two had in common was their desire to win.

   With Rodman working the boards, Robinson concentrated more on

AS A YOUNG BOY, DAVID ROBINSON DREAMED OF ATTENDING THE U.S. NAVAL ACADEMY. After all, Robinson was a U.S. Navy brat (his father was a naval officer), he loved math and science, and the Naval Academy was known as one of the country's most prestigious institutions of higher learning. But Robinson never planned on becoming a basketball star. "I didn't care if I played basketball at the Academy," he later said. "I just wanted to get good grades and fit in." Yet as a senior, he was a unanimous selection as college basketball's Player of the Year. During his professional career with the Spurs, Robinson proved himself unlike any other center in NBA history—tall and strong, yet as quick and agile as a small forward. Physical attributes were not the only traits that made Robinson a rarity. He was also a gentleman and one of the greatest philanthropists in all of sports, giving back more than his share of wealth and time to the San Antonio community. "The Admiral" was inducted into the Basketball Hall of Fame in 2009.

scoring points. The 1993–94 season marked the first time in NBA history that two teammates achieved the scoring title (Robinson, with 29.8 points per game) and the rebounding title (Rodman, with 17.3 boards per game) in the same season. Robinson also made history by scoring 71 points in a game against the Los Angeles Clippers, becoming just the fourth player in the NBA ever to break the 70-point mark. Still, the Spurs failed to get out of the first round of the playoffs.

The next season, Robinson was named the NBA's Most Valuable Player (MVP). The Spurs posted the best record in the NBA, finishing 62–20, and then made the most impressive postseason run in team history, winning two playoff series before succumbing to the eventual NBA champions, the Rockets, in the Western Conference finals.

Strange forward Dennis Rodman was a rebounding dynamo, leading the NBA in boards per game seven seasons in a row (1991–92 to 1997–98).

CHAPTER FOUR

THE TITLES ROLL IN

Despite all of the Spurs' talent, the NBA Finals remained beyond reach. In the 1995 off-season, San Antonio decided to make some changes. Although Rodman's rebounding and tight defense were valuable, his odd and often hot-tempered behavior disrupted the team's chemistry, so the Spurs traded him to Chicago. They then brought back Sean Elliott and obtained veteran point guard Avery Johnson. The changes didn't translate into immediate postseason success, though; the Spurs fell to standout forward Karl Malone and the Utah Jazz in the 1996 playoffs.

A crafty leader nicknamed the "Little General," Avery Johnson played for four other NBA clubs before becoming a starter for San Antonio.

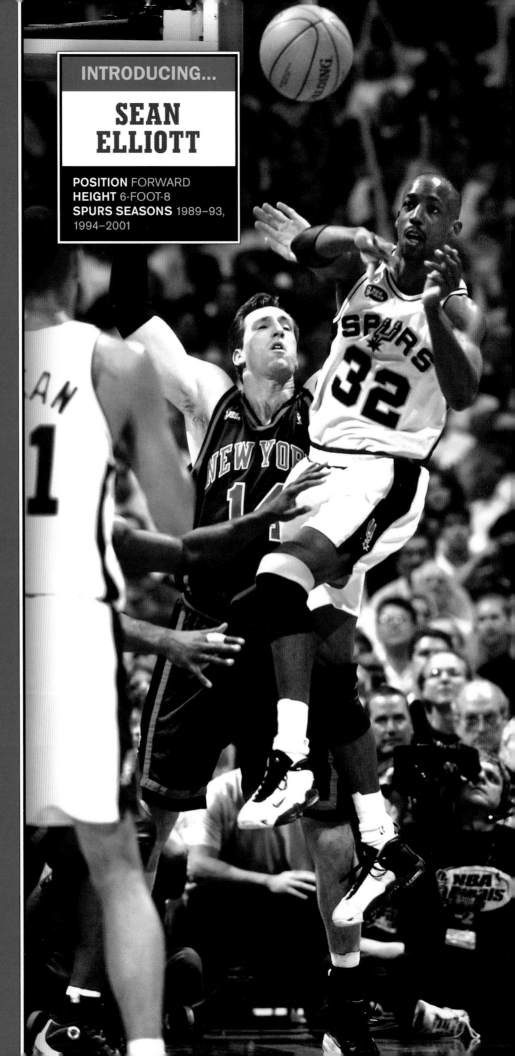

SEAN ELLIOTT WAS NICKNAMED "THE NINJA" BECAUSE WHEN HE PLAYED DEFENSE, HE SEEMED TO BE EVERYWHERE AT ONCE.

He brought out his most lethal moves, however, on the offensive end of the court. The best example occurred in Game 2 of the 1999 Western Conference finals. The Spurs trailed the Portland Trail Blazers by 2 points with 12 seconds remaining. Spurs guard Mario Elie threw an inbound pass that sailed wide and was nearly stolen by Portland forward Stacey Augmon. Elliott nabbed the errant pass before it went out of bounds, pirouetted on his tiptoes, and nailed a 21-foot jump shot over the outstretched arms of 6-foot-10 forward Rasheed Wallace. Elliott's shot turned the momentum of the series in the Spurs' favor, and San Antonio went on to win its first NBA championship. On March 6, 2005, the Spurs retired Elliott's number 32 jersey. "This is a humbling day," said an overwhelmed Elliott. "When I came to San Antonio 15 years ago, I never would have dreamt that some day my number would be hanging up there with players like George Gervin and David Robinson."

INTRODUCING...

SEAN ELLIOTT

POSITION FORWARD
HEIGHT 6-FOOT-8
SPURS SEASONS 1989–93, 1994–2001

I n 1996, Spurs general manager Gregg Popovich moved to the bench
as the team's new coach. Popovich proved to be a popular leader, but
the Spurs were decimated by injuries. Robinson, Elliott, and sharp-
shooting forward Chuck Person all missed the majority of the season,
and San Antonio finished with a disastrous 20–62 mark—the worst
record in franchise history. The lone bright spot was the play of 37-year-
old forward Dominique Wilkins, who, in the twilight of his career, finished
the season as the Spurs' leading scorer with 18.1 points a night.

That horrible season turned out to be a blessing when the Spurs
were awarded the top overall pick in the 1997 NBA Draft. Again, as
in 1987, they used it to select a center—Tim Duncan from Wake
Forest University. Like Robinson, the 7-foot and 260-pound Duncan
was extremely agile and excelled not through flash but through superb
fundamental skills. And like Robinson, the young center became an
instant All-Star. "Once he gets more comfortable, he's going to be unbe-
lievable," said Robinson. "He can score on the block, he's got great post
moves, and he's a great passer."

WHEN THE NBA NAMED GREGG POPOVICH THE 2003 COACH OF THE YEAR, THE HONOR CAPPED OFF A LIST OF IMPRESSIVE AND UNLIKELY ACCOMPLISHMENTS.

Popovich earned a Soviet studies degree and played basketball at the U.S. Air Force Academy in the late 1960s before going on to coach and teach at a small California college. In 1988, he was hired by the Spurs as an assistant coach, and in December 1996, Popovich took over as the Spurs' head coach. Coach "Pop," as San Antonians affectionately called him, quickly earned a reputation as a fiery taskmaster. "A lot of bad words. He gets all red, and he screams right at your face," said guard Tony Parker of Popovich's coaching style. "Sometimes I think he's crazy." But as abrasive and demanding as he could be, Coach Popovich was just as devoted and playful, fostering a close-knit atmosphere within his team. "I've never been on a team where the coach says 'know something about your teammate,'" explained forward Robert Horry, "because if you [do], he becomes part of you. He becomes like family."

INTRODUCING...

GREGG POPOVICH

COACH
SPURS SEASONS 1996–PRESENT

With Duncan—who became known as "The Big Fundamental"—
inserted into the lineup as a power forward, San Antonio leaped
to 56–26 in 1997–98, a 36-game improvement over the previous
season that surpassed the franchise's NBA-record 35-game turnaround
of 1989–90. The next season, the Spurs were virtually unstoppable.
Robinson, Duncan, and backup seven-footer Will Perdue formed a towering frontcourt. Elliott and guard Mario Elie provided consistent outside
firepower, while the speedy Johnson served as floor general.

Coach Popovich guided this talented lineup to a league-best 37–13
record (the season was shortened to 50 games due to a labor dispute
between NBA players and owners). In the 1999 playoffs, the Spurs
destroyed the Minnesota Timberwolves, Los Angeles Lakers, Portland
Trail Blazers, and New York Knicks, losing only two games total en route
to their first NBA championship. "Defense won it for us," said a jubilant
Robinson. "This championship sends a message that persistence and
hard work can pay off."

David Robinson throws down a dunk during the 1999 NBA Finals.

CHAMPIONSHIP CHEMISTRY

IN 1998–99, THE SAN ANTONIO SPURS FINALLY FOUND THE PIECES THEY NEEDED TO CAPTURE AN NBA TITLE. Over their first 22 years in the NBA, the Spurs enjoyed spectacular regular-season success, including 10 division titles. They'd suited up legend-ary players such as forward George Gervin and center David Robinson, who won scoring titles and the NBA MVP award. And they'd boasted perhaps the loudest, most loyal fans in the league. But until point guard Avery Johnson sank a baseline jumper to secure a four-games-to-one victory over the New York Knicks in the 1999 NBA Finals, the Spurs had failed to bring a title home to their beloved San Antonio. It seemed fitting somehow that Johnson, who had been cut twice previously by the Spurs, put San Antonio over the top. There's no doubt that the dominant, towering duo of Robinson and second-year for-ward Tim Duncan were the driving force as the Spurs trounced opponents 15 games to 2 overall in the 1999 post-season. Still, the Spurs' title required the right combination of players such as crafty veteran guard Mario Elie, smooth forward Sean Elliott, and the resilient, 5-foot-11 Johnson.

Three competitive but ultimately unfulfilling seasons followed. Duncan claimed the 2002 NBA MVP award, but the Spurs returned to their old pattern—winning in the regular season and losing in the playoffs. At the beginning of the 2002–03 season, the Spurs moved into a new arena, the AT&T Center, then they started making serious noise in the playoffs again. Duncan put up 23.3 points, 12.9 rebounds, and 2.9 blocks per game to win his second league MVP award, and the Spurs captured another NBA championship, topping the New Jersey Nets in the 2003 Finals. The title took on special significance as it sent Robinson into retirement on top. Robinson ended his stellar career as just the 27th NBA player ever to score more than 20,000 points and collect 10,000 rebounds.

COURTSIDE STORIES

THE RODEO ROAD TRIP

A rodeo cowboy atop a bull.

EACH FEBRUARY, THE SAN ANTONIO SPURS EMBARK ON A THREE-WEEK ROAD TRIP KNOWN AS THE "RODEO ROAD TRIP," WHILE THE AT&T CENTER PLAYS HOST TO THE SAN ANTONIO STOCK SHOW AND RODEO. The Spurs have consistently played well over this yearly stretch. In 2003, they set an NBA record for the longest single road-trip winning streak with eight games. Over the years, the rodeo trip has been a turning point as the team prepares for its annual push to the playoffs. "We try to use the rodeo trip as a silver lining, to try to come together and realize it's tougher on the road," longtime coach Gregg Popovich said. "You get a little bit of a bunker mentality, a little edge. It's a good measure of where we are and what has to be done by the time playoffs come. We look forward to that challenge." The road trip often sends the Spurs to eight or nine cities from coast to coast, and it's not unusual for the team to be welcomed back by the strong smell of cow manure in its home arena.

CHAPTER FIVE

THE NEW GUARDS

After the Admiral's departure, two young guards, Tony Parker and Manu Ginobili, replaced Robinson as fan favorites. Thanks to their hustle and smarts, the consistent production of Duncan, and the big-game shooting of forward Robert Horry, the Spurs found themselves in the NBA Finals once again in 2005. The championship bout unfolded as an exciting, seven-game battle with the defending champion Pistons. After the third quarter of Game 7 ended in a 57–57 deadlock, San Antonio took control. Spurs guard Bruce Bowen, a defensive specialist, shut down star Pistons guard Chauncey Billups, and on the offensive end, Duncan wore down Detroit's physical defense, scoring 17 points in the second half. San Antonio surged ahead to win 81–74 in front of its home crowd for its third championship in seven years. "You follow your leader," said Parker of Duncan, who was named Finals MVP. "Timmy is the leader of the team, and he just carried us tonight."

Tony Parker improved swiftly after joining San Antonio at age 19; by 2006, at 23, he was already an All-Star and NBA champion.

The Spurs strengthened their championship roster further in the off-season by signing fleet-footed veteran forward Michael Finley. But the 2005–06 season belonged to the ultra-quick Parker, who paced the team in both points and assists. The Spurs set a franchise record with 63 wins, but in the second round of the playoffs, they fell in overtime to the Dallas Mavericks in a nail-biting Game 7.

San Antonio finished the next season as the hottest team in the league. The Spurs won 25 of their last 31 games, then rode that momentum all the way back to the NBA Finals, where they faced rising star forward LeBron James and the Cleveland Cavaliers. The Cavaliers had no answer for Parker, who sliced apart Cleveland's defense with his quickness and precise passing. San Antonio easily swept the Cavaliers in four games to claim the 2007 championship, becoming only the fifth franchise in league history to win four or more NBA titles.

The 2007–08 campaign was the Spurs' 35th overall, and they flexed their muscle again, advancing to the Western Conference finals before losing to the Lakers. Over the next two seasons, Duncan, Parker, and Ginobili led the charge again, while newly obtained forward Drew Gooden and such up-and-comers as forward Matt Bonner and guards George Hill and Roger Mason Jr. provided solid support. San Antonio finished

COURTSIDE STORIES

HORRY IN THE CLUTCH

Robert Horry holds the Spurs' 2005 NBA championship trophy.

AS OF 2010, FORWARD ROBERT HORRY WAS THE ONLY PLAYER OUTSIDE OF THE 1960S BOSTON CELTICS TO OWN SEVEN NBA CHAMPIONSHIP RINGS. And the fact that he won them playing for three different teams—the Houston Rockets, Los Angeles Lakers, and San Antonio Spurs—made him only the second player (after forward John Salley) in NBA history to do so. Although never a regular-season star, Horry earned a reputation as a big-game, clutch shooter. "Big Shot Bob's" first game winner came as a member of the Rockets in Game 1 of the 1995 Western Conference finals against the Spurs. During its 2004–05 championship season, San Antonio took full advantage of Horry's steady marksmanship as he made 38 of 85 three-point attempts in the playoffs, nailing a buzzer-beating "three" for a Game 5 win over the Detroit Pistons in the NBA Finals. As sportswriter Marc Stein put it, "No one as far down the star scale as Horry has been this steely cool and clutch in playoff crunch time for so long and so often and in so many different uniforms."

INTRODUCING...

TIM DUNCAN

POSITION CENTER / FORWARD
HEIGHT 7 FEET
SPURS SEASONS 1997–PRESENT

TIM DUNCAN DID NOT GAIN RENOWN WITH HIGH-FLYING ACROBATICS OR MONSTROUS SLAM DUNKS; HE DISTINGUISHED HIMSELF WITH TECHNICAL BRILLIANCE. Duncan earned the nickname "The Big Fundamental" because he had a countermove for every form of defense that opponents threw at him. His quickness and agility were deceptive because he was always in complete control of his movements. That body control could be traced back to his childhood as a competitive swimmer in St. Croix, the U.S. Virgin Islands. In his early teens, Duncan made a name for himself in the international swimming community. With incredible focus, he could break down every stroke and increase his times by making the most minute adjustments. But when Hurricane Hugo destroyed all of the pools in St. Croix in 1989, Duncan decided to concentrate on basketball instead. His constant desire to improve and his ability to make small adjustments in his game paid off on the court. "Any superstar that can handle criticism and is willing to improve," explained coach Gregg Popovich, "you have a special player, because no one else [on the team] can make an excuse."

with more than 50 wins for the 10th and 11th straight seasons, but it fell in the first round of the playoffs in 2009 and the second round in 2010.

From the Iceman to the Admiral to the Big Fundamental, the Spurs have featured some of the finest big men in NBA history. They have also assembled one of the best all-time winning percentages in NBA history and built a dynasty with four league championships in the late '90s and 2000s. Most impressive of all, year in and year out, the Spurs have given San Antonio a team that never retreats and never surrenders, making it a natural fit in the "Alamo City."

The Spurs fortified their 2009–10 roster by adding two new forwards: rookie DeJuan Blair and former Nets star Richard Jefferson (below).

INTRODUCING...

MANU GINOBILI

POSITION GUARD
HEIGHT 6-FOOT-6
SPURS SEASONS 2003–PRESENT

ALTHOUGH HE WAS BORN IN ARGENTINA, WHERE SOCCER IS KING, MANU GINOBILI GREW UP WITH BASKETBALL IN HIS BLOOD. Bahia Blanca, Ginobili's hometown, has a rich history of competitive basketball. His father Jorge, a great point guard in his day, managed the Bahiense del Norte club, and young Manu was a fixture at practices and games. As a pro, Ginobili rose quickly through the Argentine and Italian ranks with his boundless competitiveness and breakneck drives to the basket. Ginobili signed with the Spurs in 2003, and as a rookie, he became an integral part of San Antonio's 2004 NBA championship run. In 2004–05, Ginobili earned All-Star status. "He's been in a lot of big games in both the NBA and overseas for years, even though he's a young guy," said Spurs coach Gregg Popovich. "He doesn't feel pressure, he relishes it." In 2004, Ginobili helped give his home country the greatest gift a basketball player can—an Olympic gold medal. Ginobili became a national hero in Argentina, a celebrity almost on par with soccer legend Diego Maradona.

INDEX